THE SWEETEST
& THE
MEANEST

ALBUMS BY TOM KIMMEL

5 to 1 (1987)

Circle Back Home (1990)

Don't Look Back (1993)

Bones (1994)

Short Stories (1999)

Shallow Water (2002)

Honor Among Thieves (with *the Sherpas*)(2003)

Light of Day (2004)

TOM KIMMEL

THE SWEETEST
& THE
MEANEST

Cover art: Marilyn Murphy
Box of Hot Ideas, courtesy of the artist

Design: Gena Kennedy

POINT CLEAR PRESS

Post Office Box 121393
Nashville, Tennessee 37212
www.pointclearpress.com
www.tomkimmel.com

ISBN: 0-9772679-1-1

for my father

CONTENTS

3. PRETTY

4. MY SPECIALTY

5. SHANGRI-LA

[1] A poem by Tom Kimmel's sister, Molly Fleming, written in response to
"My Belly"

[2] A poem by Tom Kimmel's sister, Molly Fleming, written in response
to "Sneezer"

ACKNOWLEDGEMENTS

No artist works in a vacuum or lives long in this world with his or her heart intact without the grace of inspiration and the encouragement of peers, friends, fans or family, and I've been blessed with all of the above.

I am especially grateful to Kenneth Robinson, whose friendship, kinship, teaching and artistry have made me a better man and certainly a better poet. His fine collection of poems *The Year of Lovemaking and Crying* greatly inspired me to explore new ground with my own writing.

I am also grateful to my mother for teaching me that words are magical. Dylan Thomas, in *On the Words in Poetry,* wrote of his love of the sounds of words when he was read to as a child, even before he could grasp their meaning. My mother's readings of poems and stories enthralled me when I was a young boy, and I sometimes feel something of A.A.Milne seeping through as I write and read today. *Of all the Knights of Appledore, the wisest was Sir Thomas Tom....*

To the fans of my music, who have requested poems along with the songs, whose repeated inquiries about this book-in-the-works encouraged me to finish and publish it—I am grateful.

For several weeks in the summer of 2004 the Nashville Public Library made available to me an excellent private space for work on this book, and I am grateful to Susan Earl and to the library staff for their courtesy.

My wife and daughter, Robin and Ellen Andrews, have been unfailingly supportive through the joys and disappointments of my ongoing endeavor to make my living doing what I love, and this means the world to me.

Bonnie Smith was invaluable as my editor here. She stepped in with a clear eye and big heart when I most needed someone to help me pull this book together. She laughed and cried in all the right places, and her strong hand and soft touch are evident throughout. I owe her a great deal.

I am also grateful to Terri Stewart, my booking agent, for sending me out into the world; to Kari Estrin, for encouragement and career advice; to Marilyn Murphy for allowing me to feature her work on this book's cover; to Kent and Patti Freeman for steering me to Lightning Source; to Alyce Yarborough for *Catcher in the Rye*.

I am blessed, too, with many dear friends who remind me year in and year out that what I create is of value, even when the rent is overdue and it seems that no one else is listening.

And I am blessed by the spiritual communities that welcome and nurture me: the worldwide Siddha Yoga community; St. Augustine's Chapel in Nashville; the strong-hearted circle of the Yoga for the Emotional Body community; St. Andrew's in Mountain Home, and all the churches and spiritual gatherings that invite me to share music; the Kerrville Folk Festival, Uncle Calvin's Coffeehouse, the Bluebird Café, Anderson Fair, the Listening Room, and like communities around the country and the world.

I am grateful to Gurumayi, Reta Lawler, Thomas Huffman, Matthew Fox, Thich Nhat Hanh, Linda Manning, Ram Dass, Becca Stevens, Mark Forrester, David Yarian and all the guides, teachers, patrons and mentors who have taught me to free fall and dig deep and lighten up and *feel* what there is to be felt in this world. Feeling it, and going with the feeling, the place opens that makes room for poems and songs.

Finally, I am grateful to my large, loving, colorful family, whose encouragement—and, often, forbearance—is essential to me. I beg your forgiveness for poetic license; I ask for your continued blessing, and I offer you my love and heartfelt gratitude.

PREFACE

Someone asked me recently which I enjoyed writing more, songs or poetry. "Poetry," I replied. "Because you can't make any money at it."

Over the past several years I've increasingly given myself reign to follow my impulses to write poetry, and correspondingly to share many of those poems in concerts. Over time the poems have become as important to me as the songs, and it's been gratifying to have fans request readings or copies of certain poems.

Although I've long thought of poems (including prose poems) as being musical—as being like songs in their content, flow, sound and feel—I've also recognized that poems and songs are different artistic species. Rarely would I attempt to adapt a poem to music; when a poem comes, it comes on its own, with no need of melody for support.

I've never been a very technically minded songwriter. Though I can manage talking construction and technique, and I enjoy teaching the occasional workshop, I believe that ultimately words and music, artfully married, register only in the heart, the body, the seat of intuition. So it's been a joy for me to discover my voice as a poet, to find that place in myself that recognizes a poem when it's asking into the world, beyond the realms of criticism or commerce.

As the Mystics say, something arises from nothing in the field of luminosity, and when it's had its day, dissolves again. For me, there's contentment present in the wake of a beautiful or urgent or poignant thing passed, if it came honestly and was let go of when it had come to its fullness. From what I can tell, the ability to sense this is a pure gift, something an artist can hardly earn and will certainly squander without feeling great gratitude for it.

When I began to summon the nerve to write poems—and to share them, and to call myself a poet—I found that I tended to demonstrably mimic whoever I was reading at the time, and I must admit that while reading Sharon Olds, Wislawa Szymborska, William Stafford and other poets I've written a fair-sized pile of stuff that will never see the light of day. I began to understand, thankfully, that for better or worse I had to learn to ignore my need to prove anything or to find acceptable themes or forms, and to instead begin to serve the impulses that sought expression from my own experience, feelings, longings and stories.

So here it is, the first sharing, and I offer it with gratitude and respect.

CANNIBALS

THE SWEETEST AND THE MEANEST

An old girlfriend said to me once,
You are the sweetest man I've ever been close to.
But you're also the meanest.
You're the sweetest and the meanest.

Later I thought to myself,
Well then I'm true to my own people.
Isn't that how we are,
the sweetest *and* the meanest?

Maybe our meanness is what makes it possible
for us to be so sweet; maybe the sweetness
is simply necessary to offset the meanness,
to make it bearable.

I prefer to think, however, that it's the
other way around—that we're so sweet,
so naturally, innocently sweet, that
we can't bear it, so it's our meanness that
becomes necessary, becomes our lifeboat,
our means of survival.

We don't say, *You broke my heart so*
I think I'll write a poem about you. We say,
You broke my heart so I'm going to have to
kill you—as in shoot you dead—or more likely to
simply hate you and talk dirt about you for the rest of your life.

Or if we can't get up the nerve to kill,
perhaps we'll be forced to drink ourselves to death.

At any rate, in my opinion there's
a lot of meanness down here that never
gets traced to its source. It gets buried,
or sent to prison, or shut up in the house
drinking itself into the grave
while the curtains fade,

but it never gets called what it is:
the backside of sweetness
—a sweetness that's so close to heaven
that it's almost intolerable here on earth.

CANNIBALS

My grandmother's name is Helen,
and her sisters, Ida Mary, Cornelia and Frieda;
but to the family they are affectionately known as
Bubba, Mamie, Nee Nee and Tu Tu.

I tell my Yankee girlfriends
before a family wedding or funeral,
*Listen, no amount of Steel Magnolias
is going to prepare you for this.*

Just before I leave for
a whitewater kayaking adventure in Nepal
my grandmother calls and says,

"Tommy, your mama tells me you are going to Nay-paul."
Yes ma'am, I say, I am.
"Well," she says, "You are not going."
Now Bubba, I say, I am going.
"No," she says, "You are not."

Bubba, I say, I've got to go. I've made plans.
"Well," she says, "You can change 'em."
I'm sorry, I say, but it's too late for that.

"Now Tommy", she says, "don't you defy me!"
I say, *I don't want to defy you.*
"Well then," she says, "don't do it!"

*Bubba, I say, I don't want you to worry.
I'm going with good people,
and I'm going to be very careful.*

After a long, uncomfortable silence,
she says, "Well then, you just
stay away from those cannibals."

THE MAN ON THE PHONE

My dad is not a crier.
Like most men of his generation,
he's always put his game face on
when things get touchy.
I don't mean that he can't
express affection; he can.
We get a hug coming and going,
and he'll say *I love you* and mean it,
but he's rarely lost his composure,
and when he has, it's usually been in anger,
with a loud voice, harsh words
and maybe a slammed door.
But when his little terrier Willy
got into the rat poison
he wailed like a woman at the Wall.
My mother phoned each of us
in Nashville, Memphis and Tupelo
and had us talk with him.

Afterwards we conferred and expressed
our amazement, because he had sobbed
until he was unintelligible, and
when we could catch a phrase
intact it would be something like,
"He was just my little boy," or
"He was the best friend I ever had," or
"You know how much he loved
to ride in the truck." Then he'd
break into a howl of grief,
which was surreal to us.
It wasn't that we didn't feel for him,
I don't mean that at all, or that
we didn't grieve for Willy, because
we all adored Willy. We'd just
never seen our father carry on like that.

After the initial devastation, over
a period of days he gradually returned

to something resembling his normal hard-assed self.
Something resembling it, I say, because I don't think
he's ever been quite the same. Or maybe
he is the same; maybe it's just that I think
of him a little differently—because these days
when he loses his temper, or stalks off
in a huff, I remember the man on the phone,
and it's a good thing. It's helpful.

MAYBE FROM THE BACK

My grandmother is the ruler
of the small assisted living home
where she resides.
I do believe she is loved and respected,
but there is no doubt
she is also feared.
The residents and staff know
where she stands on all issues.
Her dietary preferences are clear,
and her disdain for
institutional food is no secret.
"These old people," she says,
"can't eat anything."

One aide, a redhead named Cynthia,
is for some reason
particularly fond of *Miss Helen,*
as my grandmother is called at the Manor,
and Cynthia attends to her needs
well beyond the call of duty.

One day when I am visiting,
Cynthia knocks to summon us to lunch.
My grandmother, who refuses
to use her walker, even after
several falls and various broken bones,
jaunts ahead of us down the hall.
Thinking we are out of earshot,
Cynthia leans toward me,
cups her hand over her mouth, and whispers,
"Tommy, look at her. Can you believe it?
She looks just like a teenager."

Without breaking stride
my grandmother calls back over her shoulder,
"Maybe from the back!"

NICEY

I pick up the phone; it's Bubba.
"Nee Nee has lost her mind!" she says;
and I know from her tone she's not suggesting
that her sister, my great aunt Nee Nee, is senile.
"What's she done now?" I ask.
"Well," says Bubba, "she's got Nicey
eating with her at the dining room table."

"No kidding?" I say.
"No!" she says. "Nee Nee said to me,
'Helen, it's just the two of us in the house now,
and I don't see any reason why Nicey
should have to eat in the kitchen by herself.'"

"Well I'll be," I say. "That's something.
And that's upsetting to you?"

"Of course it is," she says. "Nee Nee wasn't raised
like that. And you know, Tommy, I love and
respect black people as much as anybody,
but you just don't eat with the help!
Nee Nee knows that, and I told her
how I felt about it."

"And what did she say?" I asked.

"She said, 'Helen, I'm sorry you feel that way,
but I'm too old to care what anybody else thinks.
One night I just asked myself,
*Why is Nicey eating in there when
we could be enjoying each other's company?*
Besides, we're both Democrats.'"

BUDDY

My cousin Buddy, I was told, was something of a wild Indian when he was a boy, always flirting with disaster and staying one step ahead of incarceration. And as an adult he had a fair amount of overgrown kid in him and always looked to me like he was up to something.

When I was a kid he'd stay with us when he'd pass through town, and I always liked him; everybody did. In his company, I think everyone felt like they shared with him some very important unnamed secret.

Once when he was visiting, he showed me a pistol he had in his suitcase, and he even let me hold it. I remember the rough texture of the wooden grip, and the smooth blue metal, cool to the touch. Mostly I remember it as being huge and surprisingly heavy, not like my toy guns.

Even when Buddy was still living he was sort of a mythological figure. He told my cousin Frieda that he used to swim Mobile Bay to get to work every morning, and that he carried his dry clothes in a coffee can strung around his neck, and she believed him.

And once he told me that he wasn't really Buddy, but was an army friend of Buddy's who had taken Buddy's place at home so Buddy could work undercover for the government behind the Iron Curtain.

Buddy dropped dead on a tennis court when he was forty-four, and everybody still misses him. Rarely at a family gathering is his name not brought up.

Sometimes now, as a grown man, I feel a little bit like Buddy, because the family doesn't quite know what to think of me. They got over worrying about me a long time ago, but they're still not exactly sure what I do, or where I am most of the time, and they'll pretty much believe anything I tell them.

Plus I can tell they love me, really love me, because they seem so pleased when I come around.

MY FATHER

My stepfather is my father now
and has been for forty years.
I recall the time when he was Uncle Gary
in the way a hypnotized subject might recall
amazing scenes during a past life regression.

I recall, too, how after a brief honeymoon,
he and I began a war that damn near
killed me, and for all I know
nearly killed him too.
And I care not to detail his
sins or mine, for as a
new walk-in-the-door father
myself I'm now seeing
shapes emerge from a gauzy world
I'd ignored or overlooked:

He claimed me. He claimed me
when no one else did, when the
one who started me fell away from
my life like a spent booster rocket.

And by God he paid the bills,
he came to the football games,
sympathized with the teachers,
sent me to camp, invited
me (as a grown kid) home at Christmas,
imparted his impossible-to-heed advice;
adopted me and my sister to make us
a family. He explained the infield fly
rule, taught me to catch and clean trout.

All these things rest
softer in my heart these days,
but the softest, the gift that
touches me in a place I may never
show him, do not as yet have the
courage to share

with him, sitting in his boat,
riding in his truck, is this one:
from Day One he called me
his son—not stepson, stepkid or
Wally's Boy, his adopted pain-in-the-ass—
and he introduced himself,
and has for all these years now,
as my dad. *Hi, I'm Tom's dad.*

THE PIG

A New York native,
friend of mine,
noted that when he asks
for directions in pretty much
any small town in the Deep South,
invariably there will be a reference
to the Piggly Wiggly.

*Just go on down 2 blocks past
the Piggly Wiggly and turn left.*

*Oh, it's easy to find,
it's right behind the Piggly Wiggly.*

Or, *Well that's right across the street
from where the Piggly Wiggly used to be.*

As for me, mention of
the Piggly Wiggly invariably summons up
the Alabama of my childhood,
and I can hear my great aunt Mamie saying,
*Well some staples are cheaper at the Piggly Wiggly,
but the produce is better over at Greer's.*
And my grandmother's voice, clear as the morning:
*Now I mostly shop the Red & White
because they let you sign the ticket,
but I do like that young butcher at the Pig.*

MA MA'S TABLE

At Bubba's behest,
they sifted through the house
and pored over the furniture,
photos, crystal and silver
once it was universally
agreed that Bubba would
indeed sell the place
and move into the little
apartment at The Manor.

Cousins' names were chalked
onto chair and table bottoms,
inked onto strips of paper
taped into drawers.

Mama called to say, "If you
don't *ask* for anything
you're not going to *get* anything."

I considered this and for
the life of me couldn't think
of a thing to ask for. Then it came to me.
"What I'd really like," I told her,
"is that prayer on the little tile
hanging next to the breakfast table."
And Mama relayed the request.

When Bubba got the message, she said,
"All right then, Tommy gets
Ma Ma's dining room table and chairs
—*and* the china cabinet.
I don't want to split 'em up."

A chilly shock wave fanned out
along the branches of the family tree:
*Bubba's giving Tom Ma Ma's dining
room set.* And soon the word
circled back around to me:

Bubba had decreed it settled, thus
prohibiting debate. "It's Tommy's now,"
she said. "Y'all have all the nice things you need."

My great grandmother's furniture—the great
claw-footed oak table with the extra leaves
to seat twelve, the matching cane bottomed oak chairs
and the fine rickety curved-glass china cabinet
had been the finest things Bubba owned,
and now they were headed to my little house at
the end of a short dead-end street chopped off
one house down from mine by the railroad track.

Those trains would be rattling
that glass as they passed, but by that time
Bubba would be ensconced at The Manor
in two small rooms that might've fit
in the den of the old house,
the house where I'd lived as a boy
and Mama and Sissie had lived as girls.
And The Manor's newest resident
would be refusing to eat, cooperate with
the help, get out of bed or take the
various pills prescribed to ease what was
politely being called her transition.

Lord,
make me an
instrument of
Thy peace;
where there
is hatred let
me sow love, where there is
injury, pardon; where there is
doubt, faith; where there is
despair, hope; where this is
darkness, light; and where
there is sadness, joy.

MY FATHER'S BRAND

In the crowded
inelegantly shabby
neighborhood grocery,
they are perched behind
the service counter
near the pipe cleaner packets,
between the pregnancy test boxes
and the cans of lighter fluid:
Trojan, my father's brand.

I remember the day
he stuck his head in my door
and said, "Buddy, you and I
are going for a little ride."

And I recall how a few blocks
down the road he produced
the empty wrapper to a spent condom,
carelessly left behind in his back seat.

I was prepared for an angry lecture,
or worse, but all he said,
as he dropped it in my lap was,
"Just make damn sure you
always use one of these."
And when my heart began
to beat again, he added,
"And try not to leave these lying around.
Your mother might find one."

Looking back of course I see
that this was damn good advice,
and I would have
done very well to heed it.

DETOUR

Driving back from the coast
we take a little detour
so I can show my new family the old house.

We drive past the school,
which has tripled in size
since I was a boy,
but I recognize the spot
in the schoolyard where I lost
a front tooth to a baseball bat.

Around the corner from the school,
the place is easy to find.
That's the first lawn I ever mowed,
I tell the girls.

The little house and yard are remarkably
unchanged, save for one thing:
a tall tree is in the front yard,
a tree that did not exist when I was a child,
and this tree somehow casts not only a shadow
but a perspective that informs me
that I am, beyond a doubt,
a middle-aged mortal man.

I view the scene as through 3-D glasses
and somehow find myself thinking of
the Star Trek episode in which the crew
visits an earth-like planet that's been
constructed of their own memories
by aliens who want them to feel at ease;

and they *would* have felt at ease
if they could have left well enough alone
and refrained from turning over rocks
and pulling up shrubs to discover they'd been
beamed down onto some kind of movie set
where a car weighs no more than a feather
and the whiskey is really iced tea.

The girls and I take photographs
of each other in the yard
—I will make copies for my sisters—
and in a few minutes we will slowly
drive away through the old neighborhood
and pull back onto the highway.

The house and tree will remain behind,
most likely never to be visited by us again,
and will only trouble me once
I've been beamed back up
to my present age, my present life.

DOWNSIZING

THE SINGLE MALT

If you must drink shitty Scotch
(as provided, for example, by an airline),
drink it with soda, and it will be tolerable.
For me, the cheapest single malt,
spirit of my venerable white ancestors,
poured over a little ice, is sufficient.

Though I imagine I could learn
to value the nuanced bouquet
of the two hundred dollar bottle,
I am (in my ignorance) content to
sip the least of the single malts
and imagine that I am King.

A lifetime bourbon man
—Tennessee sour mash,
to be precise—
I recognize, at fifty,
that I care little for it
and that I adopted the potion
compulsively, out of some
delusional allegiance to my
bourbon sipping parents
and perhaps to other colorful,
secretive trunk-of-the-car
bourbon drinking uncles,
whom I revered.

How well I remember the first
stolen sips of my father's
bourbon & ginger ale[1] on the back steps
by the patio as steaks steamed
on the charcoal grill,
the sweet tang pedaling down
on my adolescent palate.

And I suppose some neural
pathway was then established,

which perhaps explains why
I ignored the intelligence my senses
relayed for decades back from the front,
until here at the brink of middle age
I've come to my senses:
my Scottish antecedents
got it right in the first place.

Sometimes, rarely, I imagine,
a design emerges from the formless
that perfectly captures the necessary,
yet previously unmanifest,
and as such, must then be created:
the Jaguar, the Stratocaster,
the canoe, the skyscraper. . .
and, like the blueprint for the Ark
or an equation predicting a new element
or particle, the single malt.

For once, the advertisements are truthful:
earthy, wooden, silken, peppery,
hint of pear and smoke; vital,
meditative, trustworthy; the cure
for religion, balm for work
and temperance for suffering;
an immeasurable blessing, worthy
of thanksgiving, promising redemption,
demanding preservation for this lifetime,
and certainly the next: Ladies and Gentlemen,
the snake oil that actually delivers.

---

[1] *Hey Dad*, I asked, *what's the difference between Jack Black &* Jack Green*? About five dollars a bottle, Son,* was his reply.

BUCKET OF SAND

The two elderly ladies seated beside me
reminded me of the matrons of my family:
bejeweled, crisply tailored, freshly coiffed
in that once-a-week-to-the-beauty-parlor way, and
they spoke with my grandmother's Old Mobile accent.

"Says here," says one to the other,
"Valerie Bertinelli lost thirty pounds."
"Well she needed to," says the other.
"See that boy serving drinks?" says one.
"I think he's a little different."
"What makes you think so?" asks the other.
"I don't know," says the first. "You can just tell."

After ordering a Bloody Mary
the first lady turns to me and says,
"And where are you headed?"
"Headed home," I reply.
"And is that Nashville," she asks?
"Yes Ma'am." I say, "We just bought a house,
so I guess we're staying."
"How exciting," she says.
"And are you doing your own decorating?"
"Yes Ma'am," I say, "but we're kind of
at that stage where nothing really looks right."
"Well don't you worry about it honey," she says.
"You can put a bucket of sand in the middle of a room
and after while it looks like it belongs there."

POETRY AT THE ASHRAM

The young man grew up
at the ashram and is now
back on his own for retreat.

His name is Girisha,
and he asks me,
How do you write poetry?

"What do you want
to write about?" I ask him.

Well the other day, he says,
just after sunset out behind
Sadhana Kutir, there was
this real thick layer of mist
on the fields like a big
slab of gray something,
and you could stand up straight
and see over it, or crouch down
a little bit and under it was like
a whole different universe.
There was a car
coming down the drive,
and it was like its headlights were
these pale golden tunnels you
felt like you could just walk down.

"Well," I say, "Why don't you
try writing it like you just described it,
real simple and direct?"

"In the field behind
Sadhana Kutir,
mist, thick,
slab of gray air,
headlights tunneling
through the evening..."

No way, man, he interrupts.
That kind of stuff makes me sick.

WHAT YOU NEED TO KNOW ABOUT ME

Here's what you need
to know if you're going
to write a song with me:
I'm going to go nuts. I
will show up late, always,
and will have a variety
of excuses as a result of
myriad tragedies that will
have befallen me. I will drink
too much coffee and leave
my phone on for that one
essential call, taking all
non-essential calls
that ring in loudly in the
meantime. I will be
frequently distracted and will
try to distract *you* by reading
you poems and news items from
my overstuffed backpack briefcase
or by playing you bits of other
songs I have written or am
currently writing. I will knock
off early due to an emergency
and will leave important
items at your house or apartment.
Furthermore I may not be able
to remember your name when I
see you at the post office, and I may
refuse to change *my version*
of our song when your publisher
suggests a new bridge.
"The old bridge," I will say,
"is my favorite thing about the song."

MODESTY

Whatever happened to
modesty being a virtue?
Was that ever true?
Or thanks to devolution,
is chest-beating now the rule?

Hey I've had three Jack Daniels here;
I'll bet you'd like to know
how sick I am of end zone dancing,
bragging on the post game show
by guys who think their money
make them twice the man, not twice the schmo.

Now I loved Joe Namath, I loved Ali.
I guarantee the Super Bowl. Sting like a bee.
But by God baby that was poetry,
not pretending they were something that they never could be.

Is modesty a virtue? Did my granddaddy lie
when he said, "Tommy, only fools
are fool enough to try to see themselves,
or *be* themselves, through other people's eyes?"

Seems now like everybody's out there running
'round and blowing his own horn,
acting like the teeny weeny day that he was born
was Christmas, the Big Bang, or something.

Celebrity & tits & ass & money, is that it?
You think you walk on water
'cause your picture was a hit?
You wrote the stupid book, all right;
now please get on with it.

And you, you came in first, okay.
Go on and sell your Coke,
your beer, your shirt, your running shoes,
your work-out video.

I know she doesn't drive that car;
you know the guy can barely read;
you know the whole thing's gone too far.
Tone down the product placement, please!

What's that? You say it's cultural,
so why blame individuals?
I'd do the same thing in their place
for their obscene residuals?

Okay, there's truth in that, else
that would not drive me half-crazy,
make me jealous. Have I not felt
I'd be rich were I not lazy?

I'll give you that, you keep your dream,
but won't you give me this? Allow
that most of us today forget the team,
run up the score? You know, somehow,
in spite of everything
so few of us choose, anymore,
love over gold, heart over will,
know what we're really looking for,
know what we're *really* looking for,
know modesty's a virtue, still.

FASCISM

When the pilot said,
*That big peak just off
the left wing is Mount Everest,*
I began to get excited.
Well I was excited before that,
certainly; but Good God,
Everest! Lhotse and Nuptse,
and that surreal staggering
white line of Himalayan peaks!

I'd left my camera packed away
in my duffel bag, but nothing
could spoil this for me. *No way.*

Dropping down toward the town of Paro
I was like a kid at the window
aboard the only jet that
can land on the only little runway
in a nation with a population
half that of the city
where I live in Tennessee.

I pick up a copy of
the country's only newspaper;
it's a weekly.
Under the banner is Bhutan's
national slogan:

*Gross National Happiness
is more important than
Gross National Product.*

The king, a man my age,
decreed when he took the throne
twenty-five years ago
that education would be mandatory
and *free*—as is health care—and
that all classes would be

taught in English, so as to
draw Bhutan gently
into the modern world.

I learn that there is more forested acreage
here now than there was when the king
took the throne and that there are no
polluted rivers in Bhutan. Not one.

A visa, however, costs
two hundred dollars a day,
and a tourist is only allowed
to stay for two weeks.

One day my excellent adventure
guide turns to me and says,
You know, Tom, there's
a lot to be said for fascism
when the dictator is a really nice guy.

MY BELLY

I can't get over my belly, mostly
I think because I've never had one.
Yet now I find myself patting it after meals and
speaking to it as I would a friend or pet.

I remember, a few years ago, watching
a direct marketing TV ad with
my sister Molly, the time lapse photography
showing a shirtless man's shrinking
abdomen as he paced on a treadmill.

I said to her, *I think that guy looked
better before he lost weight and was
left with that flap-like protuberance!*
And now I've got a little belly myself.

This is difficult for a narcissist.
I've gone up three pants sizes, am,
God forbid, weighing in each morning, counting
fat grams, and worse yet, sucking it in in the presence of women.

The worst of it is that I'm trying like hell
to avoid admitting that this *thing*, along with
the hearing and hair loss, creeping nearsightedness,
snap-crackle-and-pop-joints and

short term memory loss, is here to stay, and that
no amount swimming, speed-walking,
dieting and worrying is likely to bring reality
into alignment with my antiquated image of myself.

YOUR BELLY[1]

I like your belly
and all that it holds:
softness and kindness,
compassion and gold.
The middle of you,
your center, your heart,
your *hey, loosen up!*
—a reminder (in part)—
a signal, a beacon,
your friend through the years,
it's carried so much:
your pain, your fear.
I like your belly
and welcome it here.

Hey, Bell, have a seat.
Take a load off.
What's new¿
Say what¿
He's a tough nut¿
And he doesn't want you¿
Hang in, Bell o' boy,
I don't buy that crap.
He's a nut all right,
but he loves his new lap.

---

[1] A poem by Tom Kimmel's sister, Molly Fleming, written in response to
"My Belly"

SNEEZER

I am a violent sneezer.
My sneezes, which come in volleys
of three, four, five or more
(the record being eleven—*Yes!*)
are so ka-POW! So
like chuffing coughs
fired from a handgun
that I have been accused
of faking them.

I might hear *Bless you!* a time or two,
then perhaps *My goodness!*
Or *Wow!* But eventually
someone will say, *Come on!*
Or maybe, *Yeah right!*
Or even, *This is getting ridiculous!*

I have discovered, however,
that while I can sneeze into
a napkin or shirt to dampen
the shock of the detonations,
stifling a sneeze altogether
can result in choking or
a very painful release
through the ears.
Thus a sneeze wave breaking
during a film or funeral
can be quite dangerous.

I have also noticed that
as I get older the number of
these sneezes firing in succession
is mysteriously diminishing.
A good chain now will consist of
only four or five sneezes,
whereas not so long ago
it would be seven or eight.
As a consequence,

I'm beginning to doubt that I'll ever
reach the lofty heights
I once effortlessly attained.

I can't say I regret it,
as I imagine the world is becoming
an increasingly friendly place
to fellow diners, pedestrians,
air travelers and innocent bystanders,
but I suspect it's a less colorful world
than it formerly was,
at least in my vicinity.

SNEEZER II[1]

I, on the other hand, am partial to sneezes of quite another order:
No ka-POWS! No ka-BOOMS! No shake-down-the-rooms.
I am a sneezer from the Anything-to-Pleezer Colony of Wheezers.

Pleased to meet yer.

And we hail from a land very different from thine.
Our sneezes are delicate, and while urgent, refined.

Our emissions, unlike yours, don't disrupt or cause fusses,
though they often unravel in flurries and flushes.
One or two, three or four, five or six, they may number,
but not loud enough to disturb a light slumber.

One might expect polite support from a witness;
a *gesundheit!* or *bless you!* would certainly fit this
parade of sneezettes, these miniature missiles;
but no, they are greeted with questioning gazes,
with smirks, with *come on's!* and with brushy brow raises.
What was *that?* Not a sneeze! Yes, they frequently doubt
it is real if it whispers. Must a full-fledged sneeze SHOUT?

I tell you it doesn't; that notion is false!
My sneeze is not less than yours simply because
yours can shake the high rafters and rattle the glass.
See, *the bigger-the-better's* a thing of the past!

Hark! friend, I must say to you—and to your kind—
with your blustering, thunderous emissions in mind:
Hey shush, keep it down! Must you wipe out the room?
Your sneezes are weapons! They spew and spray doom.
Nothing friendly about them; no, they're bombs in disguise,
and, frankly, offensive to my ears and eyes.

My wheeze is a sneeze, let there be no mistake—
though you question and ponder if each one is fake.
Nay! Nay! I declare. Be it known far and wide
that a Sneezer lives here with discretion, and pride.

[1] A poem by Tom Kimmel's sister, Molly Fleming, written in response
to "Sneezer"

BLINK 182

In the window seat beside me
on the flight to New York
sits a boy of perhaps twelve,
a thin, pretty boy with a thatch
of spiky blond hair.
Judging by his designer backpack
I imagine he is taking
that look as far as his upper crust
parents or private school will allow.

He is wearing headphones,
listening to the CD player in his lap
for the first hour of the flight,
carefully changing CDs
a couple of times.

I am in a good mood,
needing a shower, having
barely made my flight, as usual.
I am wearing my Titans cap
and a sleeveless flannel shirt,
thinking I look unusually young
and hip for man my age.

When the boy removes his phones again
I introduce myself and ask
what he is listening to.
"Blink 182," he replies.
"Are they good?" I ask.
"Yeah," he says. "You've
never heard of them?"
"No," I say. I tell him,
"Hey I'm a musician, too. I've
made some records. In fact,
I've got one right here.
Would you like to hear a song?"

Without looking up
he raises a slender palm
toward me and says,
"No thanks."

.

DOWNSIZING

No one moves into a smaller place.
It's anti-American!
And moving into a smaller place
with less closet space—
Am I not undermining democracy,
being a detriment to capitalism?

What is this? Some kind of subliminal
recognition that I'll never be King?
Or am I simply getting an early start
preparing for the golden years?

Then again, how do I expect the market
to recover if I'm not out shopping?
And how can I be sure my country
will remain a superpower if I'm
paying down debt and saving money?

I'm thinking now of how during
the last wave of civil rights unrest
in Alabama, thirty or so years ago,
I was informed that I could be one
of four above-average students
at Wilcox County High School
who would be allowed to skip their
senior year, provided I was willing
to lifeguard at the town pool over
the summer *and* complete a
self-study economics workbook.

This study, to be honest,
was a fairly dry exercise,
but the workbook contained
one fascinating lesson: *A country's
fiscal well-being is eternally tethered
to an ever expanding economy.*

"How," I asked my supervisor
when I turned in my workbook,

"can growth be limitless on
a planet with finite resources?"

"Well," he replied, with a pinched
look, having quickly flipped through
the pages of my workbook
without really looking at them
and scrawling a big red letter *A*
on the cover, "It's possible, Tom,
but they can't really get into
that in high school economics."

And now, now I'm thinking of the
ever expanding universe, the galaxies
moving away from each other
at faster and faster speeds
into cold, infinite space,
like subdivisions disappearing
into the south Alabama countryside.

PRETTY

MORE LIKE THE DEVIL THAN DANA COOPER

First I left for a year, then a year became two.
Three and four became five, became six, like they do;
and Ruelene must have thought I had left there for good,
but I knew I'd return to that place when I could.

In the fullness of time I set off down that track
to find out for myself *you can never go back,*
down the rail and the highway, in the snow and the rain,
till I stood at her door in my hunger and pain.
Her eyes glazed over, she fell into a stupor.
I looked more like the devil than Dana Cooper.

Now Dana Cooper was a man with a blank for a past,
which we filled with suspicion and rumor.
There was talk of a wife and a bone-handled knife,
but no one in this town ever knew her.

Seldom seen in the light, he did business by shadow of night,
like a chill that passed through here; but when I came to town
that obsession with him turned to me, and I found it peculiar
when the talk filtered down of this drifter, this loser
who looked more like the devil than Dana Cooper.

Well he was not a big man, and he stood on a box
when his picture was taken. He wore mismatching socks.
But he looked quite imposing that night on the train
in the smoke-filled half-light of the late poker game.

He was cheating, but no one was calling his bluff.
One by one they all folded till finally it was just us
at the table, his shadow and me—
a Colt in his pocket, a card up his sleeve.

Then he dealt off the bottom and slipped in his Ace;
I called him a liar and a thief to his face!
He looked shocked—even shaken—and he stood in his place.

He went for his piece, and I went for his throat;
we went down to the table, then crashed to the floor
as the crowd circled 'round us to wait for the kill,
and they danced and they shouted and carried on till
the *report* of the gun! I could picture the rest....
Then I realized it was *his* blood on my chest.

First he called out to Jesus for help from above;
then he called out for her, said he'd wasted her love,
said he needed her now like a cold hand a glove,
like a lamb needs the shepherd to gather him up,
like a bird needs the sky, like a wound needs a suture....
Then I knew the devil had plans for his future.

I walked back to the Pullman, his body still warm,
tossed out my shirt to the first hint of dawn,
left the window wide open and washed myself clean,
stared into the mirror at no one I'd seen—
for the eyes of the Witness met the eyes of the *Doer.*
I looked more like the devil than Dana Cooper.

MY CAT

I have a cat.
My pride and joy, he is,
if the truth be known,
and no one likes him but me.
Oh they will say he is handsome.
Who could deny it?
—a big red tail-less cat
with high haunches
(must be Manx blood)
and a proud head
with inquiring, seeing eyes.
He'll stare you down,
which, though interesting,
is not the problem.

It's the stalking,
the nips and scratches
and relentless quest for food on
undefended plates and countertops,
and the way he bullies
his baby sister, who (by the way)
I have tried to give away
a number of times
just to spare her
his constant aggression and
general overbearing attitude.

"Why don't you give *him* away?" they ask.
Well, it's not because
no one would have him
(which is true),
but because I couldn't bear
to part with him.
You see, sometimes
when no one else is watching
he climbs into my lap
and becomes the burned,
chainsaw-loud purring red kitten

begging for scraps under my feet
in the courtyard where I found him.
And in those moments,
when we're together in that way,
all is forgiven:
I know I love him,
and he knows he's loved,
and I cannot blame him for
his difficulty discerning the difference
between playing and fighting,
between kissing and biting.

PRETTY

Pretty's not the word.
Her face, you can see all its parts,
but not at the same time.
That is to say, there is no
overall effect of it; or rather
the overall effect is that of
looking at a puzzle; and like
looking at a puzzle, maybe
you can squint a bit and lose
the lines between the pieces,
or let your gaze soften in a dim light
and see the whole, forgetting
for a moment how it was pieced
together. And interestingly enough,
she *was* pieced together, both
figuratively and literally. Figuratively
because against all odds she found
her birth mother living in England
and was then welcomed home
by her mother's parents and cousins
to a farm in Tennessee;
and literally, because as a young woman
she survived a terrible car crash and was
pieced slowly, excruciatingly, back together.

Hers is a Humpty Dumpty face
that by a miracle, became
almost but not quite whole again,
so the whole-making for her had to
happen from the inside out and press
itself into outside forms, into outside
puzzle pieces: pieces of songs into
songs, pieces of color into paintings,
bits of blood and bone into a woman;
pieces of love into a heart.

Now look at her again, more closely.
See what I mean?
Pretty's not the word.
Beautiful is the word.

CAB RIDE
(ROUND TRIP TO ISLIP)

I.

Look, why don't you just let me take you all the way to the city?
You take the shuttle to the train, that's five dollars. Train's like ten
dollars, plus you can't make the 6:09, so you gotta wait outdoors
for the 7:15, then you got to take a cab from Penn, that's what?
twelve dollars? fifteen dollars, depending on where you're stay-
ing? So you add all that up you're talking thirty dollars. You split
the cab, it only costs you ten dollars on top of what you're
already in for, you save an hour and a half, I take you right to
your door.

What do you say?

II.

Six degrees of separation—
that's like a real word? I thought I made it up.
So is that like an anthropological term?

I took Anthropology 101, but
I didn't make it back for the next one,
if you know what I mean.
It was hard, let me tell you,
really hard—all cultural and social,
nothing physical whatsoever.
We had to read *Survival of the Fittest*
and understand the whole thing
—everything—which I figure makes me
as smart as the professor.

But what I want to know is,
why do I have to be as smart as him
just to take the class?

III.

Ronkonkoma?
Oh, that's an old Indian word.
It means *the lake out by the airport.*

HIPPIES

I watch the construction workers in my neighborhood
disembark from their vehicles,
long hair beneath ball caps
streaming ponytails down their backs.

They sport scraggly, untrimmed beards
below sunburned faces,
looking for all the world like the most radical,
dope smoking, acid dropping
back-to-the-earth hippies of my youth.

As I drive past I imagine them saying,
We are bound in many ways.
Here are ways we are free.

TANJA

Tanja told us her mother came
to the United States for health reasons,
but that her father remained
in Sarajevo during the war.
One night a shell exploded
near his apartment and blew away
everything but the concrete
skeleton of the building.
Even the wooden frame
around the bedroom mirror
was gone.
Mercifully he was out at the time,
but everything he owned was lost.

She said to us,
One of the hardships of the war
was that the city was without water
and electricity for three years.
At one point, a shell hit the National Library,
and it caught fire.
Since there was no water
there was nothing anyone could do.
People stood in the street and watched.
My friends told me the ash rained softly
for three days, and you could still
read the words of the books in the ash.

for Tanja Softic

DOWNTOWN

I play the coffee shop
to six people, three
of whom are working
the show and another
running a loud blender
in the back of the room.

Another audience member
was my opening act, and
after my set he follows me back
to the greenroom, a cluttered box
in the back of the building
that is actually painted
a psychedelic shade of green.

"It's not you," he says.
"It's this town. It's pathetic.
Did you see that mess outside?
They're putting in sidewalks.
Why? I ask you. Nobody comes
down here anymore. I mean
nobody. They put a cemetery
downtown just to get some
people down here. Hey I was at
my dad's shop the other day,
and he said, 'This is *ridiculous.*'
He said he'd only seen one car
down there all morning long.
I looked out and said, 'Hey Dad!
There's another car!' And
he said, 'No, Son, that's the
same car, backing up.'"

LAWN & GARDEN

I bought five big bags of pine mulch at Lowe's today,
and the woman running the cash register in Lawn & Garden
told me how happy she was to be back there, back in Lawn &
Garden,
because she worked a promotion in Home Decorating for a
while,
where she got a commission on custom drapery orders,
except she never *had* any orders, because practically
all she had time to do was cut custom mini blinds to length.

One day, she said, she and the manager cut mini blinds
for three solid hours without having time for one single other
thing.
So forget commissions!

Out in Lawn & Garden, she told me, nobody comes out
and bothers you and tells you what to do all the time,
plus everyone out there works as a team. A *team*, she said
—like people helping each other out a little bit
every now and then. If they knew anything about that
over in Home Decorating she might still be working there,
even if it meant once in a while she had to cut a few mini blinds.

THE NAP

I am going down for a nap,
curling up like a seal
on a rock,
welcoming without craft
or even appreciation
the perfect balance of
sun and spray.
I do not care
that the decked boat passing
below me carries seasick
passengers finished off
by the hard waft
of my over-warm sea smell.

I am down for the count.
I, who have been swimming
against the tide since
time's invention,
have quit the game
and given the hopeless task
and impossible odds against
achievement to vain fools
and younger men.

Truly I am drunk with sleep.
I am in heaven.

And though the ocean
may call and call,
though supper may follow
the tide to safety
and my mate swim to China,
I care nothing for unwritten history.
Content beyond question,
I am tied to this world
only by gravity and breath,
and I am not coming.

MY SPECIALTY

WEDDING POEM

I loved you
before I had a name for it,
before I had an idea of it,
even before my first notions about it
had little to do
with what I offer you now:

my whole heart—
not without fear or reservation,
but with all my glorious misunderstanding
and human fallibility,
my misplaced allegiances,
my unfulfilled promise,
my imperfect longing and devotion
and complete willingness
to fall down this mountain with you.

If these were the greatest
treasures in the world
I'd still lay them at your feet
with roses and mornings and rivers.

for Maria & Nick in New Zealand 3/23/01

ROOM WITH A VIEW

Sitting on my bedroom floor
winded from long conversation
my friend Tom rises
to relieve himself,
the mysteries of the universe
unsolved.
Hey check this out,
he whispers from the bathroom,
waving me over.

Across the courtyard
they sit in the window,
young lovers, facing away
into their dark room,
unaware of our invasion.

Soon they kiss,
and kiss again,
with such tenderness
that we are
not titillated,
but embarrassed,
as if we are suddenly
naked together.

Her blonde hair catches
the moon; they are
silhouetted by the dim light of a
silent television within
as they move in rapture on the sill.

We speak softly in monosyllables,
our fascination stronger
than our guilt for watching.
We are twenty years older
—so close by that
a cough would startle them—
and we know the depths of the

young man's passion in
the well of our own bodies.

Go Man! Tom whispers.
Now! I say, men that we are,
past inhibition,
no woman to check us,
and he does, they do,
for they are gone from the window,
the set flickering to an
empty room.

We open beers without speaking,
return to our seats
on the floor to resume
conversation, but there
is nothing more to say.

BAD NEWS

You are bad news, girl.
Seriously bad news.
May I tell you a little story?

Once when I was living alone
at the farmhouse on Pleasant Hill Road
I arrived home in the middle of an afternoon,
and as I began to climb the front steps
to the rickety porch I heard a strange commotion
around the corner. Now you see
I kept an ever-dwindling flock of chickens,
and at this point my hens,
once a carefree sisterhood of twenty-two,
numbered only three, and for the life of me
I could not catch the predator. Of course
when I'd stayed in town late for a gig or a date
I'd lost chickens to nocturnal thieves
—skunks, possums, weasels, owls—
but now my babies were disappearing daily
in broad daylight. And this peculiar halting wail
I heard was definitely emanating from a hen.

I crept around the right side of the old house
and edged my way to the back. Peering around the corner,
I could not believe my eyes! A red fox was sitting
in plain sight on the hill behind the house, not fifty feet away,
staring intently at my obviously bewitched hen,
who was weaving her way from side to side in a wide
but narrowing swath that took her ever so slowly up the hill
directly to the fox, who seemed to somehow
be calling the unfortunate girl to him. It was like
he was reeling her in against her will
with some kind of primordial tractor beam!

Later I asked my farming neighbors
if they'd ever seen such a thing, and none had,
although my landlady said that on one occasion
she'd seen a fox sit under her apple tree
in the middle of the afternoon and eat fallen fruit.

Certainly I was witnessing a rare event.
Mesmerized myself, I watched until
my hen was maybe ten feet from the fox,
who apparently was content to wait till
she had delivered herself to his jaws.
I silently backtracked to the front door,
grabbed my old .22 rifle and eased back around
to my hiding place. Although something in me
wanted to see the ritual through, I could not bear
to see my hen seized, so at the last moment
I fired above the fox's head. In a flash he was gone
into the thicket, and within a few minutes my hen
was pecking away in the grass for grain and bugs,
oblivious to the danger passed.

The reason I share this little tale
is because it reminds me of me and you.
After each dangerous and unsatisfying encounter
I tell myself that this one was definitely the last.

Then you call to ask a small favor. Or perhaps
you simply visit me in a dream, and you're faithful
and tender. We curl up and sleep peacefully,
coffee and toast in the morning.

Listen, I concede your right to
your own nature. It's where we begin.
But the truth seems so simple
when my rationale wears thin.

If you'll never be right for me
cause you're just no damn good,
then go back, go back,
go back to the woods.

BACK TO HEAVEN

I love you like rain loves
a summer sidewalk.
I cannot stay here
but the warmth of
your rough surface,
as I embrace you
momentarily—even
as I begin to move
(rightfully, unavoidably)
toward more welcoming,
familiar ground—
changes me in the
warming, sending a
part of me back
to heaven.

GENERATION GAP

On one of our first dates
we drive to Memphis.
I play Jimi in the car,
and she loves it—
Voodoo Chile, Slight Return.
"That sounds great!" she says. "Even for now."
Oh yeah, I nod.
Even for now.

Later we're talking about
our favorite records,
and I mention The Band.
"What band?" she asks.
"The Band," I reply.
"I know, but what band?"
"The Band," I say.
"What, a band called *The Band?*" she asks.
"That's right."
"Oh," she says, "that's clever."

A few days later she calls to say,
"You know that band you were telling me about,
The Band?"
"Yes, I do."
"Well," she says, "Did you know
Robbie Robertson was in that group?"

MY SPECIALTY

Everyone needs a specialty,
and mine is unavailable women.

They can be lesbian
or they can be married,
or they can have just
fallen in love
     with someone else;

or they can be sweet on me
     but sweethearts with my best friend,
or no longer sweethearts with him,
     simply someone he'll never get over.

They can actually be available,
—*now this one's a personal favorite*—
     yet simply refuse to give me
     the time of day;
or they can be available
     emotionally but not
     available physically,
or be available
     physically and emotionally,
     but wanted by the law,
     hounded by creditors
     or mentally unstable.

They can even be perfect
     in every way and fully
     aware of our unique soul connection,
     yet bound by their selfless
     care for elderly parents or
     orphan children far away,
     perhaps on another continent.

There may be the problem of
     opposing political or
     religious ideologies,

a disapproving father
or overbearing mother.

They can be kind and giving,
    yet alcoholic or drug addicted.

There's the language barrier,
    allergies that don't allow us
    to eat the same foods,
    pets that hate me,
    pets that love me but drive me nuts,
    pets that happen to be *birds*.

A match made in heaven
    for me would feature
    at least three of the items listed above.

Just think of the poems I'd tender,
    the songs I could write.

CAST IRON SKILLET

She threw out my cast iron skillet.
I asked about it when we unpacked
the kitchen boxes and it was nowhere
to be found, and she said she might have
given it away. Might have!
Then I complained about it
on several occasions, told her that skillet
had twenty years of seasoning working on it
and that being from Chattanooga
she should've known you can't just replace
twenty years of seasoning—to which she replied
that if I'd been in town to pack my own
damn kitchen I'd have a right to complain
and otherwise shut up! Anyway,
whatever small satisfaction I got
from whining was displaced
by the sting of loss when it was time to cook.

I'd look through the kitchen cabinets
from time to time as if it might appear,
and it was like looking down a long
driveway late in the afternoon, waiting on
a wayward wife to reappear with
a good excuse—the kind of excuse
that would bring ease and forgiveness—
but of course wayward wives rarely reappear,
and if they do, never with a good excuse.

I just pray that whoever picked that skillet
up for two dollars off the table at Goodwill knows
what a jackpot they hit, and that they
went home and fried some chicken in it,
then scrubbed it out with salt, and put it away,
maybe after kissing it.

LOVE NOTES TO A PHYSICIAN

I

Lordotic curve,
you say,
lordotic meaning *curve,*
the curve of the small
of your back,
to clarify your instruction
and explain the term's
inherent redundancy.
In my ignorance,
however,
I only know
I want to kiss it.

II

Suprasternal.
Suprasternal *notch.*
Clavicular fossa.
Left, right, clavicular *fossa.*
Notch, fossa, hollow.

Touching these hollows,
I am closer to you,
closer to your heart.
And
I tell you,
touching these hollows,
how much
I love
science.

III

Healing the sick
is important,
and in no way
would I
underestimate
its value.
But
what really knocks me out
is the way
you raise the dead.

COINCIDENCE

Today, Monday, I pick up my mail at the Post Office window. There's a fair size box of it, as I've been away for ten days.

I sort it on the table in the lobby, tossing the junk pieces in the trash.

A pretty woman paying bills at the other end of the table calls my name and comes to give me a warm hug. I've not seen her in years. *Jennifer*, I say, pleased that I remember.

She is looking through her mail and we chat. She asks if I've been abroad lately. I tell her not since last year. *And you?* I ask. *Do you travel abroad?* She says she's been performing in Russia—music and missionary work—and names the cities.

I am making little stacks: magazines, bills, solicitations. And here, between my Greenpeace renewal and the frequent flyer statement, is a letter addressed to Jennifer. Jennifer Martin. Without speaking I hold it out for her to see.

We are startled, clearly.

She takes the envelope and opens it. *Look*, she says, holding up its contents—a handwritten note and folded one hundred dollar bill — and she tells me it's a thank you gift for a recent performance.

She does not say, however, that this must be a sign from God, and that we should spend the money on dinner and a movie, or maybe give half to the church and buy a great bottle of wine with the rest and drink it by the fire at her place—it's turning wet and cold today. No, instead she says, *Well thanks for the letter,* and walks toward the line for stamps.

Have a nice Thanksgiving! I call after her. I walk to my truck in the cold drizzle, not hurrying, and write this down.

WALKING BEHIND YOU

God must have retired after
She created your *behind*. I do
believe it's possible because I've
practically lost track of the Almighty in my
pursuit of your well-rounded bottom.

Then again, maybe God is still in
business because clearly I'm in heaven
walking behind you up the stairs to
my apartment. You are self-consciously
aware of my attention, yet you allow it,
work it a little, for five glorious flights.

And to think how I once complained
of carrying water or groceries, or
cursed at forgetting something, racing
back up in bounds, freshly showered,
breaking a new sweat, rattling the old lock,
bounding down again to the idling car.

You have graced this stairwell with
a fluid beauty unseen in its eighty years
—or my own forty. Someday we will
leave this place, but I pray I will always
follow that hallowed motion.

ILLUSIONS

I love you, and I know it, though I'm sure I don't know why.
Maybe we just need to love the ones we never had to try
to love. Lord knows you don't deserve it more than anyone else
does.

But the fact is I adore you like the law adores the truth,
and the rain adores a river; the sun adores the moon.
And I've no idea how this could be
after everything I've done to you, and all you've done to me.

See, I have no illusions; if we were somehow to agree,
I know what (in agreement) I would be agreeing to:
letting you pretty much run wild, my love,
and taking care of you, being pleasantly surprised
if you were faithful, somehow faithful,
and occasionally—I'm smiling now—threw in a buck or two.

And the point is, I imagine, and the reason why I called,
is I love you. I just called to say I love you. That's all.

BOOKS, THE MORNING AFTER

I've heard you can tell a lot
about people by their books.

Browsing her library
the morning after while she
showers upstairs, I see

Terms of Endearment
A Confederacy of Dunces
The Secret Garden

And what's this?

Clyde Edgerton
Pat Conroy
Amy Tan

Hmm.

Atlas Shrugged
Gone With the Wind
The Stand

The Stand?

Then a shelf of John Grisham.
What's *that* about?

Leon Uris
Kerouac
Wallace Stegner

The Hobbit!

She calls from
the top of the stairs:
"Push the button
to start the coffee!"

And now the oversize
coffee table books:

Masters of Impressionism
Edward Hopper
Norman Rockwell

Cezanne
Picasso
Pollock

Frank Lloyd Wright
Rivera
O'Keefe

R. Crumb!

THE REAL THING

I'm sorry but
this is vile and undrinkable,
this coffee.
No amount of sugar
makes it sweet.
The air in this cabin is
sandpaper in my throat;
I'm on the row of seats
that won't recline,
and the other ear doesn't work
in *this* pair of headphones
—not that I want to watch
Autumn in New York
again anyway.
You, Ma'am, are quite possibly
the only redeeming feature
of this cross country flight.

Oh but you—what a feature!
You say you gave up
teaching kindergarten
to be a flight attendant
so you could escape
Chattanooga, Tennessee.
My Lord! With your
perfect ponytail and your
starched white airline blouse,
you look like a cheerleader,
like a porn site Lolita,
like the girl who carries
the cross down the aisle
in my mother's church.
And look at that fine
blonde fuzz over your lip
when you turn your head
that way in the light;
that may be the most beautiful
sight I've ever seen.

What in the world is it like
to get out of bed
every morning knowing
you have lips like that?
And you say you've been
on the job just three months?
You're a baby!

But then, look at your klutzy walk,
your trembling hands,
your unaffected smile.
Hey that's no toothpaste ad!
It's the *real thing*—
which is to say,
dear God,
you are the real thing.

Innocent.

Well, you don't need me
staring at you, do you?
No. I mean yes.
Yes! I *would* like more coffee,
with extra cream please.
Oh thanks—that's plenty.
How kind of you to ask.

HONEYMOON AT FIFTY

A honeymoon at fifty,
    our second (on the average);
quiet, and gray to
    accentuate the autumn foliage;
four days to set our precedents
    as lovers, partners, friends;
a welcoming beginning,
    a blessing at the Inn.

SHANGRI-LA

GAI

On the long flight from LA to Bangkok
I could've been seated amongst the horde
of Japanese businessmen, or next to
any number of fellow passengers
who would've ignored me as I read, dozed
and half-watched a series of in-flight movies;
but I was seated next to a pretty young Asian woman
who tapped me on the shoulder and introduced
herself as Gai, an exchange student traveling
from college in Colorado home to Thailand
to care for her ailing mother.

"Excuse me," she said, "may I see the book you are reading?"
I pass it to her; it is called *Shambhala,* and I tell her
she can keep it for awhile as I'm going to watch
the film, which is about to begin.

Two hours later I remove my headphones,
and to my amazement she has devoured
the book and is eager to talk about it.
"So surprising," she says, with an earnest smile,
"that a Westerner would be reading this book."
I assure her that many Westerners are reading it,
that it is widely available and fairly well known.
"I would like to find out," she says, "if a translation
is available in Thai. If not, I would like to translate."
I tell her I will send her a copy; she immediately
reaches for her bag and says, "I will give you money now."

Later she taps me again and says dreamily,
"You know, West and East are so different.
In West, all culture, all social and spiritual models
emerge from Descartes' axiom, 'I *think,* therefore I am.'
In East, however," she continues, "all culture,
all social and spiritual models flow from the understanding,
'I *breathe,* therefore I am.'"

Then she curled up and slept into the long night.
I, however, was quite awake, and would
not be sleeping till the next evening.

SHANGRI-LA

Today, my first full day in Bhutan,
Joan and I walk the trail
from ancient Punakha Dzong
to the put-in on the Po Chuu,
between the tumbling river and the fields of waving farmers,
startled children shouting,
through woods that look
for all the world like North Carolina.
Our trail is often just a foot's width dent
in the steep face of a red hill
or a slippery vertical slope down
into a creek, up suddenly on the far side
toward the treetops, the high forest floor.

I stop to photograph archers competing
in a field across the river, and in the process
of juggling water bottle, camera and lenses
I unwittingly drop my *mala*, my prayer beads.
Discovering my folly some ways
down the path, I know it is too late
to retrace my steps and retrieve it.
"You must feel doomed without your mala," says Joan.
Eying the rushing blue river below,
I say, "Please, any word but *doomed*.
Frustrated, disappointed, sad—crushed, even.
But not doomed."

Another mile on the winding trail
delivers us to the porters and drivers
waiting with a horde of ragged children
and the other members of our group.
The big gray raft and my bright blue Redline
are strewn with my fellow paddlers'
yellow and red Overflows
in a jumbled pile along the rocky shore.
I casually finish outfitting the Redline,
climb slowly into my dry suit
and notice my fatigue, the dizzy tightness
I tell myself is the altitude.

As Joan and the rafters pull away she waves
and calls, "See you at the bottom!"
"No, no, please!" I yell back.
"Not at the *bottom,* at the *take out!"*
But it is too late; the raft is barreling downstream.
She can't hear me.

I wedge myself into the Redline
and am whisked away with the others,
my new companions *Doomed* and *At the Bottom,*
stowed below deck, whetting their dark appetites.

MANGDE CHUU

I am standing on a large grey boulder
on the shore, river left, studying
the monster chute in front of me,
and Allan, our superb British guide,
is saying to me, *"See,* there's the line.
From the big rock in the center up top,
you peel off high and start the drop
right against the wall. Ride it like a train,
and it'll take you all the way down."

And what about that giant hole
at the bottom?

"It's nothing," he says. "If you're
too far right it'll munch you pretty good,
but it won't keep you.
About the time you think
you're done for it'll spit you out,
and if that happens, just roll up
and eddy out left below it."

"Here," he says, "watch Land run it."
And we watch his Mississippian counterpart
glide across the horizon line above us
to catch the tongue off the top wall.
His boat kisses the rim of the fall
and he is instantly rocketing
down the long cascading ramp.
A few seconds later he's a hundred yards
downstream, smiling in the eddy,
having seemingly never
tensed a muscle.

"There you go." says Allan. *"Piece of cake."*
Noting my obvious incredulity
he says, "Look here, Tom.
Forget everything but the line.
None of *that"*—meaning the chaos

before us—"concerns you."
And then I was seeing it,
the line, clear as day.
And I know two things.
One: I've never before
run a rapid this big; and
Two: I'm going to run this one.

STONE'S

Used to be a place
near Cleveland, Tennessee,
called Stone's Truck Stop
—now just a crumbling shell and
eighteen-wheeler parking lot—
and the waitresses there
looked like they'd been
cryogenically preserved in
the last seconds of a hard life;
but the chopped steak,
after a long day on the Ocoee
—smothered in gravy and
onions—to die for, and
no unsweetened tea on the menu,
thank you very much, just
tea the way God intended,
with more ice than tea and
enough sugar to strangle you;
and they had a killer jukebox
with all the right stuff: Ray Charles,
Alan Jackson, AC/DC, Hank Williams.

I'm guessing that would have been
enough to lure most patrons
—hard core truckers,
from what I could tell—
but strangely enough there was also
a *doll shop* tacked on to the far corner
of the building. And I'm talking
the finest, pale little handmade dolls
with flowing hand-stitched dresses
and delicate porcelain faces
—for the truckers to take home
to Mama, would you say? Shelves
and shelves of the dainty creatures,
all of a bygone era, real collectors items.
And who made them? Who loved them?
And who, by the way, sold them?

Because there was always
a velvet rope across the door to the shop
and no one at the counter inside.

But here's what's most memorable
to me about Stone's: tacked to the wall
by the kitchen door there was a
big poster depicting a shrouded
Christ holding up a sorrowful looking
young blue-jeaned working man who had
collapsed backward into
Jesus' arms. Looking more
closely you'd see that the boy
held a large mallet and spike
—the nail holes apparent in the Lord's hands—
and the ground was strewn with lilies
and crisscrossed by a stream of dark blood.

The first time I saw it I was
caught by surprise and had to
steel myself quick so my
fellow paddlers didn't notice
I'd begun to tear up.
I shut it down fast,
and on subsequent trips
I'd be prepared, would even
show it to new friends as a
quaint curiosity. Still it somehow
always got to me, and now
when the memory arises it comes
with that sad pang of surprise
and the wish that I had
the courage to trust
the things that make me cry.

CRIPPLE ME

Pierce's songs, they cripple me.
They cut me deep and leave me open,
unable to collect myself.

My Guru cripples me.
My mother cripples me.
If a woman doesn't cripple me
I would rather be alone.

I don't want to be healed;
I want to be touched.

I don't want to be comforted;
I want to be loved.

I don't want a crutch;
I want a clear path to the altar.

SADDER THAN JESUS

President Kennedy was shot
five days before my tenth birthday.
My teacher, Mrs. Primm,
solemnly informed us,
first that he'd been shot,
and just a little later
that he'd been killed.

My mother cried her eyes out,
cried for days, cried like
I'd never seen her cry before,
like I'd never seen anybody cry.
She and I sat on the foot of the bed
in our house on Bigger Street
in front of our little black and white
television, and we cried together.
Then I knew beyond a doubt
that the world actually contained
such sadness: the casket in the
Rotunda, the riderless horse,
the caisson, John-John's salute,
and Caroline—she and I
had the same birthday,
so I could imagine how sad
she must have been.

I remembered then the first great
sadness I'd felt, when my mother
had taken me on her knee
and explained to me about Jesus,
about how He was God's beloved Son,
and how He had given his life for *me*,
so that I could live, and how he had been
the best man in the world, even
the best man the world had ever known;
but that he had been *betrayed*
by a friend of his, for money.

And she'd told me that even though
God loved Him more than anything,
Jesus had suffered on the cross,
nails right through His hands and feet,
and that He'd hung there
until He died; and I had cried;
I'd sat right there in her lap and
bawled until I was breathless and asked,
"Why? Why? *Why* did he have to die?"
And she'd said, *"For you.* He died for you—and for me."

And that was sad, it was sad
beyond belief or understanding,
sad enough to make a boy embarrass himself
in his mother's lap; but now I knew
that sad as it was, this was even sadder,
because President Kennedy was dead,
and it was sadder than Jesus.

LOST CAUSES (2003)[1]

I have a friend from Iowa. Grew up on a farm. Big Yankees fan.
I said, "You know, Randy, that's like pulling for Goliath."

I am a lover of lost causes.

Once a certain evil recording
engineer in New York said to me,
"I've finally figured out how
someone from Alabama could be
such a big Red Sox fan.
It goes hand in hand
with losing the Civil War!"

Well he can go to hell on
both counts, and I'm certain
he will. And don't you think
he'd already have to be living
in some soft corner of hell
to even conceive of such a thing?

Tell me, what if Jesus had hired
a bodyguard? If Buddha had opted
for a medical solution? What if
Robert E. Lee had accepted
Lincoln's flattering offer
and burned Virginia?
If Rama had stayed home
and enlisted a band of mercenaries?

What if Hanuman, a free agent,
had signed with the Yankees?

Can I know love if I have not
suffered loss? Joy if I've not
bathed in despair? Peace if I've not
made at least one deal with the devil?
And how can I call myself honest
if I've never once sold out my brother?

The Guru says never fill your
stomach. All hunger, she says,
is hunger for God. And in
Fenway Park, the bellies are
never full. It's been so long since
they were filled it's like
it's simply never happened.
But the longing, it's so very sweet.
It's the sweetest longing
in the world.

[1] In 2004 the Boston Red Sox won the World Series for the first time in
eighty-six years.

I AM NOT A POET

Poetry is something I cannot do;
that's why I have to try.
I can write a song—they come along
and I write them—but a poem...
I am in awe of a poem.

I have nothing to say to a poet.
If I did, I'd tell him, "Hey I'm a poet, too."
But it wouldn't be true.
I am in a state of what you might call *Aspiring Poet,*
which is a kind of purgatory.
Not too bad, but it won't yield a poem.
But perhaps this is the Guru's kindness,
because if I wrote a poem my pride could swell,
and I might lose perspective.

Wishing for a poem keeps me hopeful.
Hopeful keeps me honest.
Honest keeps me tender, and
Tenderness makes poetry seem possible.

Perhaps someday I will become a poet,
but if it happens, I imagine it will happen
like the volunteer morning glories in my garden.
Without strain, there's one and there's another.
And there's enough water, enough light.
No one invited them or welcomed them,
but there they are, making themselves at home,
like poems on the pages of a book,
on the pages of a real book of poetry.

EULOGY

I am not going to stand here in front of
friends and family and say he was
a good man; not when we all know
our late friend was not particularly so.

He had his good days, certainly,
and his good qualities: the ability
to catch fish when he should
have been working comes to mind;

the way he was able to keep
his liquor hidden from his wife
and appear sober at AA meetings;
that's notable, definitely;

his uncanny knack for winning
money from his buddies, knowing
they would bet their hearts on certain football
teams, against their better judgments;

plus we should not overlook
his gift for exaggeration
in successive tellings of
tall tales and off-color anecdotes.

But a good man? Is it not
goodness enough that we loved him?
That he was not an especially
good man, and we loved him?

MY SISTER

My sister Helen sang Christmas carols
even in the summertime;
she was weird like that.
Once she ate a whole
stick of butter. And once,
I guess because she was told
not to, she stuck her arm
right in Bubba's big window fan.
You had to keep an eye on her.

If my sister was last at the table
she would likely hide what was left
of her peas and rice under the rug,
and once a fossilized sandwich
was found in her Sunday purse.
Mama says that whereas I would
tell the truth when a lie would've
saved me from a whipping, Helen
would tell a lie when the truth
would've gotten her out of trouble.

Fact: my sister was much smaller than I was
and thus extremely susceptible to torture.

At various times I:

– locked her out of the house
   in the snow wearing
   only her pajamas

– stuffed her upside down
   in a garbage can

– placed a large dead spider
   in her open mouth
   while she slept in the back seat
   on our way to the beach.

But here's the story of the meanest thing
I ever did to her:

My sister wanted a horse
more than anything in the world.
She asked for one each birthday and Christmas,
and as every birthday and Christmas approached
she was told that Mama and Bubba and Santa Claus
were very sorry, but that you just can't
have a horse if you live in town, and so on.
Still, this was implausible to Helen and
she continued to dream as she played
with her toy horses, drew pictures of horses,
wore her cowgirl outfit, pretended to *be* a horse,
wrote Santa faithfully each year
(starting around July), till one Christmas morning
when she was six and I was eight, I had a terrible idea.
I ran to the back window and yelled,
Helen! Helen! Look what's tied to the tree!

        *   *   *

My sister has long since
forgiven me for this and for countless
other crimes and trespasses,
but I can tell you without a doubt that
I have not forgiven myself
for this particular transgression.

Therapy and prayer have alleviated other regrets,
but somehow I still imagine myself before the Judge
being told, *Son, there's a difference between
a practical joke and a sin, and there are sins
for which there is no remedy, for which penance
is ineffective—for certain acts set worlds in motion
that will spin eternally, worlds of dark secrets
from which you will never be free.*

These days, when the family banter starts up
about our childhood pranks and follies

I inevitably remember that Christmas morning,
and if the story is told I hold my breath and sweat it out.

So my prayer now is not for the gift of remorse.
I have that; I've had it for years now, certainly.
What I need is no less than a re-write of history,
a chance to undo what began with great force.

I imagine a world where dark fact becomes fantasy,
and fantasy fades from a gray sky to blue—
where a wish is a seed taking root in reality.
Merry Christmas, dear Helen, may your dreams all come true.

LET MYSELF IN

I pull down your driveway.
It's two a.m., the dog knows me,
does not bark.

I climb the steps.
The pet rabbit on the deck
is awake, quivering in the chair.

I have my key, let myself in,
have a bowl of cereal
in the quiet kitchen,

brush my teeth
(I have a toothbrush here)
and tiptoe up the creaking stairs.

First I slip into her room.
She sleeps as if she's been
etherized. Probably I could

stroke her hair unnoticed, but I am
afraid, and anyway I just want to
watch her as I would a museum display.

Nine years old she is, going on thirty-nine,
a baby when she is dreaming,
and all yours. No, that's no longer true;

she is now the tiniest bit mine.
You too will be heavy with sleep,
but you will stir when you hear me in the hallway.

ABOUT THE AUTHOR

Tom Kimmel's songs have been featured in film, in television and on albums by dozens of artists, including Johnny Cash, Joe Cocker, Randy Travis and Linda Ronstadt, selling millions of copies and achieving gold and platinum sales in countries around the world. A recording and performing artist in his own right, he tours widely and has released seven albums. Born in Memphis in 1953, he grew up in Alabama and now lives in Nashville with his wife and daughter. This is his first book of poetry.

Printed in the United States
139152LV00002B/1/A